HAGGADAH
COMPANION

Meditations
and Readings

Alden Solovy

Kavanot Press

For information regarding permission to reprint material from this
book, please e-mail your request to: info@kavanotpress.com.

Special discounts are available on quantity purchases by
synagogues, churches, hospitals, hospices, other medical and
religious organizations, associations, corporations and others.
For details, contact the publisher at the e-mail address above.

Published by Kavanot Press, USA

Cover and text design by Bookwrights

Manufactured in the United States of America

First Printing, 2014

Library of Congress Control Number: 2013958336

ISBN: 978-1-940353-26-5

FOR MOM

CONTENTS

INTRODUCTION

One year, just before the seder, my daughters placed an empty chair at the table. With Passover beginning at sunset, the shiva for Ami *z"l*—their mother, my wife of 27 years—abruptly ended. According to Jewish law, the start of Passover marks the end of shiva, even if seven days haven't passed. We attempted to hold our usual seder in anything-but-usual circumstances, setting the table with ritual items, various versions of the Haggadah, wine-stained copies of additional readings and a memorial place setting.

The idea of adding a chair isn't new. During the struggles to free Soviet Jewry, some families added an extra chair to remember Jews in the former USSR. Other families added a fourth piece of matzah to the seder table to symbolize the struggle for freedom. Today, some people still use an empty chair or a fourth matzah to remember those who are not yet free.

Adding symbols and readings to the seder fulfills the instruction from *Sefer Netivot Shalom*: "Whoever enlarges on the telling of the Exodus is praiseworthy." Some people add an orange to the seder plate, representing the inclusion of all genders and sexualities. Others add an olive, representing the hope for peace. At our family seder, we've added a fifth cup, *Kos Miriam*, the cup of Miriam, and many supplementary readings.

This *Haggadah Companion* is a resource for you to enlarge on telling the tale, providing readings that build on the traditional story and others about the journey toward personal freedom and the call for social justice. May you find meaning in these pages, joy in your seder and praise in telling and enlarging the tale.

FREEDOM

The Season of Freedom

This is the season of freedom:
Of freedom from the will of tyrants,
Of freedom from the bondage of self,
To receive God's Holy Word.

This is the season of release:
Of release from captivity and oppression,
Of release from a foreign land,
To become a nation and a people.

This is the season of redemption:
Of redeeming our bodies and souls,
Of redeeming our strength and power,
In service to *Am Yisroel.*

This is the season of freedom:
Of reliving the ancient journey,
Of remembering the treacherous path.
This is the season that calls us to stand together,
The season that summons us to God's Law,
The season that leads us home.

Egypt Inside

This I confess to myself:
I have taken Egypt with me.
I've kept myself a slave to grief and loss,
Fear and anger and shame.
I have set myself up as taskmaster,
Driving my own work beyond the limits
Of reasonable time and common sense.
I've seen miracles from heaven,
Signs and wonders in my own life,
And still wait for the heavens to speak.

God of redemption,
With Your loving and guiding hand, leaving Egypt is easy.
Leaving Egypt behind is a struggle.
In Your wisdom, You have given me this choice:
To live in a tyranny of my own making,
Or to set my heart free to love You,
To love Your people
And to love myself.

God of freedom, help me to leave Egypt behind,
To hear Your voice,
To accept Your guidance
And to see the miracles in each new day.

Blessed are You, God of wonder,
You set Your people on the road to redemption.

Breaking Bonds

To break the bonds of anger,
To live with gentle pride.
 To break the bonds of shame,
 To live with humble strength.

To break the bonds of envy,
To serve each other in joy.
 To break the bonds of guilt,
 To accept all God's gifts.

To break the bonds of fear,
To love with fullness of heart.
 To break the bonds of lust,
 To love with fullness of being.

To break the bonds of loneliness,
To receive a hand of hope.
 To break the bonds of neglect,
 To extend a hand of help.

To break the bonds of tears,
To see with awe and wonder.
 To break the bonds of loss,
 To rejoice in all God's works.

Release Me

Holy One,
Release me from judgment.
Release me from doubt.
Release me from hunger.
Release me from want.
Release me from loneliness.
Release me from despair.
Release me from disappointment.
Release me from anger and shame.
Release me with Your gentle hand
And a song of hope.
Release me with the light of Your word
And the echo of Your voice.

God of Old,
Guide me to wisdom and strength.
Teach me to break free of the chains
That I have wrapped around my own heart.
Teach me to live a life of service to others,
A life in celebration of Your gifts.
Teach me to see myself through Your loving eyes,
So that I may return, rejoicing,
To You
And Your people.

Redeeming My Life

A part of me
Refuses to forgive
Myself
For my errors, my mistakes,
My oversights and misdeeds.
How can I redeem my life from inside
This place of judgment,
Of harsh words and
Somber requirement?

God of Old,
God of Justice and Truth,
Teach me to restore my life
Through acts of love and kindness,
Thoughtfulness and care,
In support of my
Family and community.
Teach me to surrender my days
To the joy of service to others,
Of concern for this world
And the generations to come.

Heavenly Guide,
Revive me with Your light,
Restore me with Your truth,
Refresh me with deeds
Of righteousness and charity.

SOCIAL JUSTICE

Against Human Trafficking

God of the prisoner,
God of the slave and the captive,
The voice of suffering echoes across the land.
Lonely weeping in a night that never ends.
Our brothers are sold like coal
To be burned and discarded,
Traded like empty boxcars,
To haul unbearable loads of
Cruelty and degradation.
Our sisters are kidnapped and conned,
Used like empty vessels,
Their bodies abused and violated,
Their hearts and souls assaulted.

Source of comfort,
Rock of love and truth,
You call upon us to stand in the name of justice and
    freedom:
To witness against human life treated as chattel,
To fight those who trade human beings as property,
To muster our power and energy
Against this force of evil.

Bless those who dedicate their lives to human rescue.
Grant them the fortitude to battle in the name
Of the unknown, the unseen,
Those who have been forgotten.
May the work of their hands never falter
Nor despair deter them from this holy calling.

Bless those in human bondage with hope and courage.
Grant them the strength and fortitude
To face the shames and tyrannies forced upon them.
Hasten their release.
Grant them lives of health and prosperity,
Joy and peace.

Blessed are You, God of All Being,
Who summons us to liberate the oppressed.

Against Poverty

God of the hungry,
God of the sick and the homeless,
The voice of the forgotten echoes across the land.
Dismayed and abandoned in a world of abundance,
Our children, our brothers and our sisters
Are left to beg in the streets,
To find shelter in abandoned structures,
To suffer illness without physician or medication.

Source of hope and mercy,
Rock of strength and fortitude,
You call upon us to stand in the name of healing and honor,
To witness against human life ignored,
To fight society neglecting human beings,
To muster our power and energy against this plague.

Bless those who dedicate their lives to the poor, the sick and
    the homeless.
Bless those who take to the streets to offer food, clothing
    and shelter.
Give them courage and determination.
Bless those who plead on behalf of the poor before the seats
    of power,
Governments and corporations.
Give them wisdom and skill.
May the work of their hands never falter
Nor despair deter them from this holy calling.

Bless those in poverty with resources.
Release them from want.
Hasten the day of their self-sufficiency and bounty.

Blessed are You, God of All Being,
Who summons us to oppose the tyranny of poverty.

Against Hunger

God of the poor,
God of the starving and the malnourished,
The voice of grief echoes across the land.
Dismayed and abandoned in a world of abundance,
Our children, our brothers and our sisters
Struggle to feed their families,
Struggle to put food on the table,
As they watch emptiness and longing
Consume their kin,
As they watch disease and death
Encircle their homes and their lives.

Source of bounty and plenty,
Rock of compassion and mercy,
You call upon us to stand in the name of justice and healing,
To witness against indifference and neglect,
To solve issues of scarcity and distribution,
To create a world of agricultural success in every land
And among every people.

Bless those who dedicate their lives to the hungry,
Who offer food and sustenance to the needy
And who teach others to feed themselves.
Bless those who plead on behalf of the poor before the seats
    of power.
Bless those whose ideas and research will lead to new
    solutions for ending this plague.
Give them courage, determination, wisdom and skill.
May the work of their hands never falter
Nor despair deter them from this holy calling.

Bless the hungry with resources.
Release them from want.
Hasten the day of their self-sufficiency and bounty.

Blessed are You, God of All Being,
Who summons us to oppose the tyranny of hunger.

Be'chol Lashon (*In Every Tongue*)

We sing praises
Be'chol lashon,
In every tongue,
In every voice,
In joy and sadness,
With music and with love.

We seek truth
Be'chol lashon,
In every tongue,
With every breath,
In study and prayer,
With faith and with purpose.

We pursue justice
Be'chol lashon,
In every tongue,
In every land,
In word and deed,
With strength and with courage.

We study Torah
Be'chol lashon,
In every tongue,
In every generation,
In wonder and awe,
With zest and with zeal.

We are one people,
Present on Sinai,
Where God spoke
Be'chol lashon,
In every tongue,
To every soul,
To every heart,
The whole House of Israel.

PRAISES

In Praise

Hallelujah at sunset.
Hallelujah at daybreak.
Hallelujah at dusk.
Hallelujah at dawn.
Hallelujah with pauper and prince,
With beggar and king.
Hallelujah with all God's works.

This is my prayer, God of Sarah,
To declare Your glory in all things.

Hallelujah in sunshine,
Hallelujah in shadow.
Hallelujah in calm.
Hallelujah in storm.
Hallelujah in peace.
Hallelujah at war.
Hallelujah in shelter.
Hallelujah when all comfort and protection
Appear lost.

This is our prayer, God of Abraham,
To praise You every moment.
To praise You,
To sing to You,
To dance for You,
To declare hallelujah with our lives.

Sing Hallelujah

Hallelujah
A hymn of glory,
A chant of praise,
A song of thanksgiving.
Voices raised, hearts to heaven.
Lungs full and strong.
A breath, a note, a lyric, a tune.
A call of love,
An echo of truth,
Resounding with joy and praise.

Let my hopes carry me toward wondrous deeds.
Let my heart lead me toward sacred wisdom.
Let my breath lead me to majestic truth.
Let my words exalt Your Holy Name.

Hallelujah
A song of hope,
A harmony of justice,
A chorus of mercy.

God of Miriam,
Prophet who danced by the sea,
Teach me the song of life,
Of dedication and zeal,
Of wonder and glory.
Teach me to sing my hallelujah.
Teach me to live my hallelujah.
A song of righteousness.
A song of thanksgiving.
A song for the generations.

Dance Hallelujah

Hallelujah
A dance of wonder,
A dance of joy and thanksgiving.
Arms raised, hands to the sky.
Feet solid, connected to earth.
A step, a bend, a twirl, a leap.
A breath of light,
A stream of color,
Spinning toward radiance and splendor.

Let my feet lead me toward Your Holy Realm.
Let my legs carry me toward Your Divine Word.
Let my arms lift praises toward Your marvelous works.
Let my body exclaim the power of Your awesome ways.

Hallelujah
A dance of light and love,
A dance of energy and endurance,
A dance of humility and grace.

God of Miriam,
Prophet who danced by the sea,
Teach me the dance of awe and mystery,
Of devotion and ecstasy,
Of passion and praise.
Teach me to dance my hallelujah.
Teach me to live my hallelujah.
A dance of radiance,
A dance of splendor,
A dance of peace.

For Spring

Shimmering, radiant air
Alive with new warmth.
Sunshine waking the earth,
Calling the grasses to grow,
Bulbs to prepare flowers.
Winds clear the last remnants of seasons past,
Old leaves and dry branches
Making way for new life.
And the rain joins the sun to feed the land.

Bless this day, God of seasons.
Bless the spring with energy and hope.
Be present with us as we celebrate the glory of creation
Planting the land and our lives with Your gifts,
These gardens of holiness and love.

God of time and space,
May this season be a blessing and a teacher.
Make me like the sunshine, a source of light.
Make me like the earth, a source of bounty, ready to give.
Bless my days with service and my nights with peace.
Make me like a garden,
A source of beauty and purpose,
Sustenance and splendor.

PAST AND FUTURE

History

History is sacred,
Memory is holy,
Time is a blessing,
Truth is a lantern.

Source of sacred moments,
Creator of time and space,
Teacher, Healer and Guide:
Thank You for the gift of memory,
The gift that allows us to see beyond the present,
The gift that allows us to remember our past
And to remember our lives.

Thank You for the gift of vision,
The gift that allows us to imagine the future,
The gift that allows us to learn and to teach
The lessons of the ages,
The lessons of millennia,
So that we may heal ourselves and the world.

Eternal God,
Thank You for the gift of history,
The gift of ancient moments and modern tales.
Grant us the wisdom and understanding
To see history in the light of truth,
To trust the enduring power of memory
To guide us from generation to generation.

Sages

Blessed are the sages who came before.
Blessed are the sages who'll come later.
Blessed are the sages of our day.
Blessed is your heart.

For you
Dear children,
You dear sisters and brothers,
You too are sages.
The wisdom of the ages
Is in your eyes and on your lips,
In your flesh and in your bone,
In your laughter and in your tears,
Holy music that sings around you,
Radiance that dances before you,
Prayers that echo through you.

Blessed is the sage within you.
Blessed are your studies and your deeds.
Blessed is your path and your way.
Blessed is your heart.

The Season of Counting

This is the season of counting:
Of counting days and nights,
Of counting the space between slavery of the body
And freedom of the soul.

This is a season of seeing:
Of seeing earth and sky,
Of seeing renewal in the land
And renewal in our hearts.

This is a season of journey:
Of inner journeys and outer journeys
Taking us places that need us,
Places that we need.

This is the season of counting,
The season of joyous anticipation,
Of wondrous waiting,
In devotion and awe,
For our most precious gift,
The gift that binds our hearts to each other across the
    millennia,
The gift that binds our souls to God's Holy Word.

Elijah

Eternal One,
Hear our cause!
Love and gladness,
Hope and salvation,
Israel restored,
The world redeemed,
Righteousness and mercy in an age of peace.

We are ready for healing.
Nations dream of justice,
While communities yearn for wisdom.
Leaders search for guidance,
While people seek hope and comfort,
Solace and rest.

Answer us, O God, answer us.
For You are not in the wind
Or in the shattering rocks.
You are not in the earthquake
Or in the raging fire.
You are the still, small voice.

Ancient One,
God of our fathers and mothers,
Let us hear Your voice
From Your holy mountain
As in the days of old.
Send us Your messenger,
Elijah, prophet among prophets,
To announce the time of blessing and wisdom,
To herald the return of holiness,
To proclaim Your world to come.

Jerusalem: A Meditation

Jerusalem,
You are mystery and wonder,
Secrets hidden and secrets revealed.
You are beauty in the hills
And holiness in stone.

City of Peace,
Why are you still besieged by nations?
Why are you held hostage from within?
What errant flight has the white dove taken?
What mission of love and mercy
Has drawn her away from her sacred home?

Jerusalem,
You are prayers and echoes,
Questions without answer,
Yearning and hope,
Radiance and splendor,
The heartbeat of generations.

Jerusalem,
You are my journey and my destination.
You are my dream
And you are my longing.
You are my joy
And you are my sorrow.
Will you be my consolation?

Overview of the Passover Seder

This overview of the seder highlights how these readings fit into the service. Of course, you're invited to use them wherever they most resonate for you. This outline is not intended to replace a Haggadah and is not a thorough description of seder laws, customs or practices. It includes the 14 named sections, pointing out some highlights. The named sections are flush left on the page. Highlights are indented. At the seder, we see ourselves make the journey out of Egypt. We trace Jewish history and travel on the road out of slavery into the beginnings of a nation. The cover of this book illustrates a traditional Passover seder plate.

Seder Overview	Suggested Reading
Kadesh (**Benediction**)—Recite Kiddush over a cup of wine or grape juice, proclaiming the holiness of the holiday. This is the first of four cups.	History
The Four Cups—The four cups of wine or juice match four expressions of freedom used in Torah.	*Be'chol Lashon* (In Every Tongue)
Urchatz (**Wash**)—Wash hands without reciting a blessing.	The Season of Freedom
Karpas (**Appetizer**)—A small piece of parsley, onion or boiled potato is dipped into salt water and eaten after reciting a blessing.	For Spring
Yachatz (**Breaking the Matzah**)—The middle matzah on the seder plate is broken in two. The larger part is set aside for use as the *afikoman*.	

Seder Overview	Suggested Reading
Afikoman—This is a way to keep children engaged. At some seders, it's hidden for children to find after the meal. At others, the children "steal" it and ask for a reward for its return.	
Maggid (The Story)—The poor are invited to join us, and we tell the story of the Exodus from Egypt. This begins with a child asking the Four Questions and ends with blessing and drinking the second cup of wine. This section includes:	Release Me
Invite the Poor—Stating that matzah is the bread of affliction, we invite the poor to join us at the seder.	Against Poverty
The Four Questions—A child asks four questions about what makes the seder night different from all other nights.	
We Were Slaves—Begin to answer the Four Questions by stating: "We were once slaves to Pharaoh in Egypt, and God freed us with a strong hand and an outstretched arm."	Against Human Trafficking
The Four Sons—The traditional Haggadah speaks of four sons, providing instructions to the leader on teaching different types of children at the seder.	Sages
The Ten Plagues—Recite the ten plagues, recalling the suffering of the Egyptians by removing a drop of wine from your cup for each plague.	Breaking Bonds

Seder Overview	Suggested Reading
Dayenu—A song of joy thanking God for the gifts of redemption.	In Praise
The Three Symbols—Explain the three principal symbols of the seder: the lamb bone, the matzah and the bitter herbs.	Egypt Inside
In Every Generation—A statement of the core principle that each of us must see ourselves as if we had come out of Egypt.	Redeeming My Life
Rochtzah (**Wash before the Meal**)—Hands are washed again, with a blessing.	
Motzi Matzah (**Eat Matzah**)—Two blessings are said before eating matzah.	
Maror (**Bitter Herbs**)—Combine bitter herbs and *charoset*, recite a blessing and eat.	
Korech (**Hillel Sandwich**)—Enact a custom instituted by the Talmudic sage Hillel, eating a sandwich of matzah and *maror*.	
Shulchan Orech (**Feast**)—The holiday meal is served.	
Tzafun (**Dessert**)—After the meal, the *afikoman* is eaten.	
Barech (**Grace after the Meal**)—Recite grace, then bless and drink the third cup of wine.	Against Hunger
Elijah's Cup—We invite a visit from the prophet Elijah, messenger of the Messiah, by opening the door, reciting a passage and singing.	Elijah

Seder Overview	Suggested Reading
Hallel (**Songs of Praise**)—Sing praises to God. After *Hallel*, we bless and drink the fourth cup of wine.	Dance Hallelujah
Counting the Omer—On the second night, outside Israel, begin counting the days to Shavuot.	The Season of Counting
Nirtzah (**Conclusion**)—Having carried out the seder, recite a closing prayer.	
Next Year in Jerusalem—We say: "*Leshanah haba'ah b'Yerushalayim.* Next year in Jerusalem."	Jerusalem: A Meditation
Songs—Sing additional songs. Enjoy.	Sing Hallelujah

ALDEN SOLOVY is a Jewish poet and liturgist, a writing coach and an award-winning essayist and journalist. He has written more than 400 pieces of new liturgy, offering a fresh new voice of prayer. Alden is available to teach, read his work and serve as a writing coach or as a liturgist-in-residence. He also leads prayer-writing classes for adults and teens and writes commissioned liturgy for congregational use. In May 2012, Alden made aliyah to Israel, where he hikes whenever possible. He splits his time between Chicago and Jerusalem.

Jewish Prayers of Hope and Healing is rich with meditations, poetry and prayer. This collection of more than 150 entries touches the joys and sorrows of life, ranging from psalms of mourning to the hopes of fertility, from rejoicing at childbirth to fears about life with Alzheimer's disease. *Jewish Prayers of Hope and Healing* addresses issues of our day with prayers for people of all faiths. Order copies at www.tobendlight.com.

"Soulful and meticulously crafted."
　　　　　　　　—*Jerusalem Post Magazine*

"A masterful set of conversations with God."
　　　　　　　　—Rabbi William H. Lebeau

"Authentic, honest and alive."
　　　　　　　　—Rev. Dr. Margaret Benefiel

CPSIA information can be obtained at www.ICGtesting.com
Printed in the USA
BVOW02s0051040215

386229BV00002B/14/P

9 781940 353265